I0134712

Children of Silence and Slow Time

More Reflections of the Dhamma

Ian McCrorie

PARIYATTI PRESS
an imprint of
Pariyatti Publishing
www.pariyatti.org

© 2012 Ian McCrorie

All rights reserved. No part of this book may be used or reproduced in any manner whatsoever without the written permission of the publisher, except in the case of brief quotations embodied in critical articles and reviews.

ISBN: 978-1-681723-06-8 (Print)
ISBN: 978-1-928706-40-3 (PDF)
ISBN: 978-1-928706-36-6 (ePub)
ISBN: 978-1-928706-84-7 (Mobi)
Library of Congress Control Number: 2011960776

Cover and Interior Images - John Givot, www.givotimages.com

Foreword

John Keats was so struck by the bas-relief figures on a Grecian Urn at the British Museum that he adopted them in his famous Ode as his Children of Silence and Slow Time. My two children, Aiden and Liam, neither silent nor slow, are the very antitheses of still figures on an ancient artifact. Yet my boys and the Grecian figures typify the enduring universal nature of truth that prompted Keats to declare that all you need to know in this world is that, "Beauty is truth and truth beauty." The innocent simplicity of my children, their innate ability to melt, wholeheartedly, into this single moment, in essence living truthfully, echoes Keats' sentiment.

The reflections presented here are also my children, offspring of my own silence and slow time in caves, forest monasteries and countless retreats. I claim, however, no pride of ownership, borrowing and paraphrasing as I did from the likes of Pythagoras, Pascal, Nisargadutta Maharaj, Trungpa Rimpoche, Lao Tzu, to mention only a few whose writings I purposefully pilfered. So it is perhaps better to refer to these musings as my foster children, as did Keats in his Ode.

Writing poems that capture the essence of the Dhamma is akin to lassoing the wind. Though you may be very skilled with the lariat, you are doomed to failure. You are attempting to feed people by composing a menu. A wise man once said that the role of the poet is to create in a moment something to be read for eternity. Not being a wise man, I'll be happy with a few moments of your attention. Nevertheless I do offer these Reflections for your consideration with the fervent belief that from time to time they will hit the proverbial nail on its proverbial head. Someone else said that poetry is obtuse verbiage interrupted by poor punctuation. As an educator for almost two decades I can attest this is not the case here. The punctuation is spot on.

For the verbiage, I apologize. It wasn't always so. Years back a disgruntled parent arrived at my classroom after school. She began her tirade by berating me for the low marks her daughter had received on a recent essay. I said nothing. She threatened to go right to the top to see that I was dismissed from my position. Again, I did not say a word. She continued. "My daughter worked very hard on that paper and you totally belittled her efforts. She spent hours in her room. Of course, she may have been doing other things. She can be really unfocused at times. And quite stubborn. Maybe that failing grade you gave her will serve as a wakeup call. She really respects you. Anyway, I just wanted to say how much I appreciate all your work on behalf of my daughter. Thanks so much." I had said nothing during the whole transaction proving, to return to Keats again, that "Heard melodies are sweet, but those unheard sweeter still." Succinct, clear and utterly devoid of obtuse verbiage that interchange remains my best poem.

Herein is a collection of reflections which fail to reach that standard.

To S. N. Goenka,
my Father of Silence and Slow Time

The purpose of life
is to live a life
that lies beyond needing a purpose.

One does not need a reason
to love, to smile or to laugh.
Be unreasonable.
Life unfolds with a joy beyond compare
when you don't try to figure it out.
Riding a bicycle is ridiculously impossible
except when you do it.

It is unimportant how many angels dance
on the head of a pin.
Of import is only that they dance.

The world is so full of any number of things
we should all be happy as kings.
Alas, it is not so,
for even kings and princes despair.

The good news of the Buddha,
that unhappiest of princes,
is that there is no escape from this conundrum.
Things do not get better
nor is the grass greener on the far side of the hill.
The promised land remains forever a distant dream
for there ain't no gold in them thar hills.

The wealthy suffer as do the poor.
The healthy and the sick alike are miserable.
The employed are as unhappy as the jobless,
the married as dissatisfied as the single.
Wiggling out of this most noble of truths is futile.

If escape were possible, liberation would not be needed.
If the Divine Mother could kiss and make it better
there would have been no Buddha.
If Prozac, Botox and mocha lattes worked
why are you reading this book?
And if books worked,
what is the need for a second volume?

The lotus blooms only in stagnant swamps,
rooted in the mud and the mire,
its elegant blossoms floating above the putrid surface.
It too cannot escape so it chose to transcend.

In the swamp but not of the swamp.

In the jungles of Issan we meditated long into the night.
By the light of the next morning
we saw we had not been alone.
Near us, just off our walking path,
a python lay coiled.

There for days he had lain and
there for days we had meditated.
Unaware of the danger lurking so close to us
we sat untroubled and
focused on our meditation.

Now we worried.
Now we thought only of danger.
Now visions of strangulation played
across the movie screen of our mind.
Now we meditated with one eye open.

One day the python slithered deeper into the jungle.
Our relief was short lived
for we had no idea to where he had ventured
nor if and when he might return.
Now we meditated with both eyes open.

All had been fine before when
we shared the jungle in a quiet stalemate.
He did python. We did monk.
It was not the python who upset this balance
but our own fear.

When fear disturbs the balance of the mind
it arouses sleeping pythons
who venture we know not where
and whose return is frighteningly inevitable.

The aging nearly blind abbot knew it was time to choose his successor.
He assembled his most senior monks and announced a silent pilgrimage
to the Cave of the Sacred Emerald Buddha.

Speculation as to the whereabouts of the cave was prevalent
as were stories of the beauty of the carved Sacred Emerald Buddha.
But only the abbot could lead the monks there
and then only on the eve of choosing his successor.

The trek was long and arduous but at last they came to a well-hidden cave.
"Enter and let us meditate through the night
before the glow of the Sacred Emerald Buddha," instructed the abbot.

One by one the monks entered and sat down.
But no statue glowed before them. No emeralds were to be seen.
The cave was empty.
Though the monks wondered about the abbot's delusion
and his failing eyesight,
they obeyed his instruction and meditated through the night.

At daybreak the abbot told the monks that over time
many emeralds had fallen from the statue.
Each should take one fallen emerald back to their hut.
Their tradition allowed the new abbot
to return the fallen emeralds in a week's time.

One by one, the monks, some repressing a smile,
went to the front of the cave, to remove a fallen emerald.
They found only stones.
But out of respect for their aging master,
they dutifully retrieved these stones
and placed them in the hem of their robes.

A week passed
and the abbot asked for the fallen emeralds to be returned to him.
Each monk dropped his precious "stone" into the abbot's container
and then proceeded on his way.
The abbot stared at each stone, squinting in the sunlight as he did so.
He kept count.
He knew only one monk, Rahula, who cleaned the toilets, had yet to come.

Rahula finally approached.
The abbot heard him searching in the hem of his robe.
He saw Rahula remove a brilliant emerald. The abbot smiled.
"Rahula," said the abbot. "what do you see in this container?"

"Just what you asked for, Venerable Sir," replied Rahula. "Emeralds!"

"Take these emeralds back to the cave. Remember well the path you take.
You are to be the next abbot.
When the time comes to choose your successor,
select he who sees emeralds where others see mere stones."

I am not a good meditator.
I do not try very hard to focus.
I do not keep any goal in mind.
I am not determined to succeed.
I am ambivalent about my posture,
unconcerned about what my teacher thinks of me
and unmotivated to get anywhere.
I do not have visions,
have never conversed with angels
nor levitated close to them.
I do not care about getting better,
about being healed or made whole.
I speak not a word of Pāli,
have never read the Tipiṭaka
and can't distinguish Hinayana from Mahayana.
I forgot my mantra years ago.
I own no crystals
and channel only MTV.
I live in the suburbs.
I drive a Volvo.

About all I can muster is awareness.

I guess I just don't get it.

A debilitating infection laid waste
my first trip to India.
I came for enlightenment but
left with oozing sores,
done in by the heat and dust.

Back home I juiced, flushed, vitamined and brown riced
in a frenzy of fearful hope,
leaving no natural remedy unturned.
I forsook coffee, tea, sugar, meat, fish, eggs, milk, chocolate, laughter.

My dietary asceticism only made matters worse.
I found myself living a short distance from my body.
But tickets had been bought and plans made
so I departed once again for India
exhausted, weak, and resigned to die there.

In India I had no choice but to eat all manner of fried foods.
I drank chai whenever the mood stuck.
I devoured Bengali sweets.
I poured ghee on my rice.
My quest for health and de-fatted wholeness ground to a halt
and I shelved my dietary commandments.

My anxiety dissipated. My brow unfurrowed. My fist unclenched.
And I healed.
The oozing sores dried, the exhaustion lifted,
the spring returned to my step
and the summer to my face.

Suffering is not enough.

Suffering is only ennobling
when we understand that it permeates everything,
when we see deeply into its cause,
when we are sure that an end to suffering is a distinct possibility,
and when we understand what constitutes
the path that leads to this end.

Without these four noble truths
suffering leads only to despair,
producing a melancholic resignation of futility and quiet desperation
masked by a fatalistic stoicism-
a hardening of the hearteries.

Gritting our teeth in the face of this despair
grinds everything flat.

Don't turn away from the suffering.
Don't neglect or deny it.
Don't try to rid yourself of pain.
Don't hate it.

Open yourself fully to suffering.
Embrace it. Befriend it.
Immerse it in loving kindness.
Face the ten thousand joys
and the ten thousand sorrows
with bemused detachment.

Where is the Dhamma to be found?
Some seek it in isolated caves in the Himalaya or
on the plateaus of Tibet.
Others locate it in the jungles
of Thailand and Burma.
And a few are drawn to the Zen Temples
of Rynoji and Bolguksan.

It is not found here.

Some think the Dhamma is more prevalent
on extended retreats.
Some feel it manifests only
when engaged socially and politically.
Others think it resonates most purely
through mantras and chanting.
And a few scholars discover it
in verses of Pāli and Sanskrit.

It is not found there.

Moving our home near it is like moving closer to the wind.
Capturing it in a technique or a tradition is like bottling a sunrise.
Studying it is like reading the Goldberg Variations.
The truth is here, and the truth is now.
This truth is already held in your own heart.
There is no where to go and no what to do.

You are already where you need to be
and already doing what you need to do.
"Where is the Dhamma to be found?" is not the question
but rather "Where is the Dhamma not to be found?"

Meditation is staying present
to the whole catastrophe.
It is paying attention
to your own nervous breakdown.
It is making snow angels
during the winter of your discontent.

And with this open-eyed awareness,
a smile.
Always a smile.

Without the smile, the bad guys win.

Firstly everything is dissatisfactory.
Everything.

If you think poverty is fraught with suffering,
try wealth.
If you think being married is full of difficulties,
try being single.
If you think unemployment is challenging,
try being CEO.
If living in the city causes you grief,
try living in the forest.
If living in a house unveils too many surprises,
try living on the streets.
If your disease is challenging,
try another, more pleasurable one.
If you think being alone is miserable,
try moving in with your family.

The exit sign flashes red
but the theatre is empty.

During a solitary retreat in Thailand
sitting in the heat, drenched in sweat,
fending off malarial mosquitoes,
a monk opened his eyes at one point and
found a water buffalo staring at him.
He too was standing in the heat, drenched in sweat,
fending off malarial mosquitoes.

The water buffalo, the dumbest of the beasts of burden,
appeared unperturbed by the heat, the sweat and the mosquitoes.
He lacked the discernment to want life to be otherwise
or to desire to make it different.

This buffalo became his inspiration.
The monk aspired to be as content
in the Thai jungle as this beast.
The monk did not wish to know what the buffalo knew.
He wanted to not know what the buffalo did not know.

Aspire to be as wise as that dumb beast,
devoid of preference,
content with no choice,
free from wanting what is not,
and happy with what is.

This is don't know mind.
This is water buffalo mind.

A novice monk was very much taken
by the Buddha and his teachings.
Though he already had a teacher,
he asked the Buddha henceforth
to be his one and only guide.

The Buddha refused his request.
He told his would-be devotee to remain with his present teacher.

The Buddha cared not for a plethora of students.
What gain could there be if his teachings spread
far and wide if the reputations of other good men
were disparaged in the process?

Be wary if your teacher panders to blind devotees.
If your teacher points out only the shortcomings of other teachers,
take note.
Pause for a moment if your teacher demands to be your only teacher.

Are you free to sit at the feet of another?
And as the Buddha did, would your teacher encourage
you to remain there?

Follow only those you are free not to follow.

He lived in solitary retreat
high in the Himalaya above Dharamasala.
For years at a stretch he meditated
never leaving his cave.

A young monk made the arduous journey
through the mountains to his isolated enclave.
The novice paid his respects
and sat patiently waiting some response
to his unasked but obvious questions.

"I can only say, as far as I have advanced,
that the Buddha was right."
The old monk then closed his eyes and
returned to his practice.
The novice left with none of the answers he sought
but relieved of all his questions.

The Buddha gave 82,000 discourses.
In the last 2,500 years every subsequent lecture
can be summed up in those three words
"He was right."

A large forest fire destroyed everything in its path.
For days in the long dry summer it raged on.
In time residents were allowed to return.
A woman was seen sitting in the ashes of her former home.
She was weeping.
"Why did this have to happen?"

Summer typhoon struck the shoreline with a vengeance.
The force of the wind and rain
destroyed everything in its path.
A farmer was seen sitting in the remains of his house,
surrounded by fields of flattened corn.
He was weeping.
"Why did this have to happen?"

Young parents carried their infant daughter to the hospital.
A life threatening disease was diagnosed and in time the child died.
They were weeping.
"Why did this have to happen?"

Fire burns. Rains fall.
And to be born is to be one step closer to death.
The question is never why but why not.
If it wasn't supposed to happen,
it wouldn't have happened.
Kamma is merciless.

Man is not disturbed by the things that happen
but by his opinion of the things that happen.

I joined the retreat with some trepidation
due to some discomfort in my lower back.
Sitting still was difficult
so my practice entailed mostly silent walking.

After the retreat, a novice told me that
my peaceful and mindful walking
had been a great inspiration to him.
He thought I had radiated tranquility
in my every step.
A few minutes later another mendicant shared
that when he saw me walking so slowly
he could feel the pain and agitation
in my every step.

Both observations were correct.
And both observations were wrong
for the very same reason.
We do not see reality.
We see our own bias.
When we gaze into the pond, the scum we see
is more reflection than observation.

We dance round in a ring and suppose
but the secret sits in the middle and knows.

Not long after beginning to sit
they begin.
Memories of the past, hopes for the future,
the endless video loop of wrongs and retributions,
worries, doubts and fears,
begin their dance, obscuring any clear insight
and holding liberation at bay.
Your mind feels like Keith Richards' face.

Too much effort to eradicate this agitation
further upsets our tranquility and further clouds our focus.
The tighter we cinch our belt,
the bigger our head.
If we loosen the belt too much,
our practice falls down.

Moderation in all things,
we are rightly warned,
but don't over do it.

The truth is not like this or like that.
It defies description and belies metaphors.
It is more mist than rain,
more glow than flash
and more glade than forest.
We don't get it; it gets us.
We don't see it; it sees us.

I cannot look directly at the sun's total eclipse
nor can I see it if I turn away.
I can, however, experience it.
I can witness it. I can be present.

If we look for it
the truth lies far beyond the horizon.
If we don't look for it,
it is right in front of us.

Life is one continuous mistake.

It is not so much a melodrama
as a comedy of errors, in which
the Dhamma edits your personal tragedy
to evoke laughter with each pratfall.

Longchenpa said that since everything
is but an apparition,
having nothing to do with good or bad,
acceptance or rejection,
one may well burst out in laughter.

My son fell down ninety-nine times
before he walked.
Falling down, no problem.
Walking, no problem.

Gandhi wished to die
owning simply his glasses.
Thoreau sought solace at Walden Pond.
Though the world may be too much with us
possessions need not be relinquished, just possessiveness.
The world needs not to be rejected, just worldliness.

To crave to possess nothing,
to long for the life of the sky-clad ascetic
reflects a fear of attachment to what you have.
Possessions, after all, lead only to ownership;
craving them leads to misery.

Crave no thing
not even nothing.

Love is not extreme liking.

Love is not passionate but compassionate.
Love is not blind but sees everyone as family.
Love doesn't burn but cools the fires of lust.
Love is not personal but human.
Love does not patronize but empathizes.
Love emanates.
Love engulfs.
Love radiates
on rocky crag and furrowed field alike.

I can love people I don't know.
I can love people I don't like.
I can even love those I love.

The here in being here now is not a place;
the now not a moment in time.
Being here is being real and being awake;
now is nurturing an authentic presence.

'There' may seem more romantic
and 'when' and 'if' full of dreamy scenarios.
'Here' and 'now' may pale in comparison with
future speculations or past reconfigurations,
but they are all we need for liberation.

There is just here with tea added.

Before we meditate, mountains are mountains
and streams are streams.
After some time we begin to see that
mountains are not really mountains
and streams are not really streams.
And with complete liberation
mountains again become mountains
and streams, once again, streams.

Things are not as they appear to be
nor are they any different.
Even after enlightenment
the Buddha washed his bowl.

I create all my own problems.
In fact, I am my own problem.
If I watch very carefully I see
that I magnify each and every event.
My agitation, my excitement, my anger
precipitates, preconditions, predetermines
the ensuing eruption.

It is not my problems that need solving;
it is the preconditioning mind states
that need dissolving.

Solving problems is akin
to handing the Titanic's captain a cork.
Dissolving preconditions
is giving him radar.

Liam came to me this morning and shouted,
"Daddy, let's make a four!"
His excitement was infectious;
child-likeness should be the eleventh parami.

Neither immaturity nor irresponsibility,
it is a child-like wonder
at the anarchy of life;
the ability to laugh
in the face of the futility and hopelessness of it all
and bang our spoon on the soup pot of life
for the sheer joy of making noise.
Radical enchantment.

The Dhamma does not invite us
to come in from the rain
but to go out into the rain…and play.

Cultivate the child-like heart.
Enlightenment is restricted to those under ten.

Concentration
connotes a clenching of fists,
a gritting of teeth
and a pursing of lips but

Right concentration is something else again.
It is being present to the breath.
It is bare awareness of in and out.
It is the tickle of gossamer on the upper lip.

We simply attend to this breath
with the rapt attention of a young child
at his first puppet show.

Don't be afraid of fear.
The Buddha saw it not as an impediment
but as an ephemeral and enigmatic construct.
Fear creeps into the mind
on the padded feet of worry and doubt.
Once you succumb to the intriguing plot lines
and scintillating scenarios purveyed by its two cohorts,
fear has already usurped them
and deigned himself the new commander-in-chief.
Fear thrives in this milieu
like a virus in an unshielded laptop.

Smile, taking solace that you have already been through
many terrible things in your life…
a few of which actually happened.

What, me worry?

Call it clarity,
call it luminosity or
call it clear consciousness.
Many names but all connote an
unfettered, unencumbered, unhindered, unimpeded, untangled
way of seeing.
It is your face before you were born.
Find that face.
It is your heart before you attacked it.
Heal that heart.

It is the trees before they became a forest.
Clarity is cutting down that forest
harming not a single tree.

In Upper Burma, I crossed the river
and walked up the hillside.
Outside the enlightenment cave of a long departed arahant,
a lone monk stood watch
and invited me to sit a while.

The cave was small but surprisingly comfortable.
I sat for some hours
experiencing a deeper clarity than ever before.

Was this due to some cosmic convergence?
Were the spirit guides of the cave lending a hand?
Was I resonating with the vibrations of the departed arahant?

Or was the cause closer to home,
in my own simple mind,
inexperienced as I was on the Dhamma trail?

Zen mind?
Beginner's mind?

Never mind.

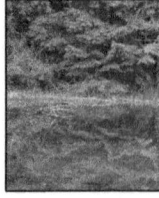

Some define living a natural life
by the number of streams that run by their home.
Returning to nature entails evergreens and owls,
loons and rock faces,
baked bread and open-hearth fires.

But within dwells the true nature
we should seek,
still inherently pure and serene,
albeit polluted by the greenhouse gas emissions
of modern life.

It is this inner nature we must redress.
Once at peace with our own true nature
we can balance our intention with our actions,
and, devoid of social pressures, live off the grid.

A babbling brook cannot soothe a raging mind
but a quiet mind can remain at peace through a monsoon's rage.

Be a light unto yourself
even to questioning the revelations of the Buddha
by holding his truths up to the mirror of your own experience,
accepting only those tenets that are reflected back.
The only truth that matters is the one that you discover.

Seek out guides not masters
for you must master your own life.
Seek out mentors not gurus
for you need principles not rules.
Seek out those who smile more than talk
for you need a change of heart more than intellectual stimulation.

The Buddha was fully enlightened
but don't trust a word he says.
Find out for yourself.
You may be completely ignorant
but you are right.

The farmer's oldest son died.
"Oh, this is terrible news," said his friends.
"Let's see," said the farmer. "Let's wait and see."

His remaining profligate son returned home.
"Oh, this is wonderful news," said his friends.
"Let's see," said the farmer.

This son was very lazy and the old man had to do all the work.
"Oh, this is terrible news," said his friends.
"Let's see," said the farmer.

The old farmer worked hard and regained his strength and vitality.
"Oh, this is wonderful news," said his friends.
"Let's see," said the farmer.

With nothing to do, the son took to drinking and gambling.
"Oh, this is terrible news," said his friends.
"Let's see," said the farmer.

War broke out but the local warlord
refused to draft the farmer's drunken son.
"Oh, this is wonderful news," said his friends.
"Let's see," said the farmer.

While celebrating his freedom,
the son fell down the stairs and broke his leg.
"Oh, this is terrible news," said his friends.
"Let's see," said the farmer.

Unable to move about, the son had to give up alcohol and gambling.
"Oh this is wonderful news," said his friends.
"Let's see," said the farmer. "Let's wait and see."

Every cloud has a silver lining and
every silver lining will eventually tarnish.
Wait and see. Wait and see.

An old monk found himself too frail and weak
to continue to work in the fields.
Because he was no longer contributing he stopped eating.
He prepared himself to die.

His brother monks came to him.
"Old man you are being very selfish," they said.
"You have stopped eating. Soon you will die.
Winter is fast approaching.
That means we will have to dig your grave in the cold.
The earth will be frozen. The wind will bite.
Have some compassion.
Eat."

The old monk was very wise.
He agreed and ate.
With the arrival of Spring
he stopped eating and soon died.

It was warm.
The earth was soft.
The winds were gentle.

All things must pass.

Eventually, you must meditate continuously
infusing every moment with clear comprehension.

And so intensive retreats are offered
to saturate the mind with this 24/7 awareness.
You sit in a silent cell for weeks, months and even years at a stretch
to etch this or that technique onto the mind
ensuring your eventual liberation.

But to depend on the twin catapults
of isolation and duration
to propel your awareness into the astral realms is folly
for you will invariably fall from grace.
Without the crutches of silence and enforced asceticism,
you will find yourself still jostled by the vicissitudes of life.

You have become a good retreatant
more than a good meditator.
Sitting continuously for months in a Tibetan cave is postcard bravado
if you cannot meditate here, now, on the Flatbush Avenue bus.

Retreat from anger, from fear, from greed,
from hatred, from jealousy, from sloth,
but not from life.
The silence we need resides not in our cave but in our mind.

If moment-to-moment awareness is the key to liberation
then clear comprehension arises when it is turned.
The former helps you to see,
the latter, to understand;
the former brings peace,
the latter, luminosity.

When each moment finds you aware,
your understanding of the human dynamic is extended
so that you comprehend more and more clearly
how change, ego and misery
permeate all phenomena.
You comprehend more and more clearly
how you constantly resist this law of nature
and crave it to be otherwise.
And you comprehend more and more clearly
how these three Sisters of Suffering
compound, confuse and convolute
the perfection of this moment.

A key is but a piece of metal.
It is only with its turning
that the key proves its true mettle.

The only truth that helps is the truth
that you discover on your own.
The Buddha liberated only himself;
and you can liberate only yourself.

But the Buddha's teachings do ease our journey
by identifying the pervasiveness of human misery.
Meditating, ask if he is right.

He identified the root cause of this misery.
Sit still and see if he is right.

He identified the state of freedom attained
once this root cause has been eliminated.
As you meditate glimpses of nibbana will prove if he is right.

And he outlined the eight stages to reach this state of freedom.
When you sit you follow these stages
and witness the results.

If we prove him wrong
he offers us a misery back guarantee.

Don't meditate.
Simply allow the state of meditation to arise.
Simply open your eyes...but keep the lids closed.
Simply see what you see...but don't look for anything.
Simply wait for it...but don't expect it.

Meditation is like waiting for the cows to come home
knowing fully well they never left the barn in the first place.

The Noble Path is not a New Age trip.

The New Age wants to heal you.
The New Age paints you as injured and incomplete
in need of some crystallized angelic convergence.

The Noble Path is Old Age.
There is no need to heal
for you are not sick.
You are not injured.
You are not incomplete.
You have not been transgressed.
You are not a victim.

You just are.
And you just are the way you are.

The New Age wants you to turn stones into diamonds.
The Old Age wants you to see things as they really are.
And when you do
you see the stones were already diamonds
and all diamonds merely sparkling rocks.

You can't meditate.
I can't meditate.
The Buddha couldn't meditate.

But meditation can occur
provided you, me and the Buddha
stay out of the way.

When you think you are meditating,
start again.

You can call it vipassana if you wish,
explain your practice as satipatthana,
tell friends you do anapana,
impress others by talking of shikantaza,
or say that you simply sit.
You may refer to yourself as a Buddhist,
a student of the Dhamma,
a layman or a monk or a nun.
You can choose Hinayana or Mahayana or Vajrayana;
Soto or Rinzai; Nying-ma, Ga-gyu, Sa-gya or Ge-luk.
You may sit on a bench, on the floor, or on a mat.
You may chant, recite, pray, or bow,

just as long as you see what is happening
and you're not upset by what you see.

This is Dhamma.
Leave the rest to the spin doctors.

If you're trying to meditate
you're not meditating.
If you think you're meditating
you're not meditating.
Even if you meditate,
you're not meditating.

But once "you" are not there,
then
you've got it...

if there is a you to get it,
and if there is an it to be gotten
and if you need to get
what you already had to begin with.

When you finally get it,
you realize it isn't it.

In upper Burma I waited
to meet the revered master.
Hours passed, dusk approached
when finally the master emerged from his hut.
He was almost blind and so beset with other infirmities
he needed an attendant with him at all times.
Yet he exhibited not a trace of remorse or bitterness.

As he touched my face,
the better to see me,
he exuded so much compassion
and unconditional love
that tears of joy filled my eyes.
He brought this confident, ego-centric, and patronizing foreigner
to his knees.

Blind, hobbled, emaciated and senile
he was the most powerful man I had ever met.

Metta can indeed move mountains;
moreover, it could even move me.

I was racked with fever
and near delirious with worry.
"Am I dying?" I wondered,
exacerbating the very symptoms
of whatever illness I suffered.

"Why me? Why now?"
eventually turned to
"Why not me? Why not now?"

And for this I had no answer.
If not me, then who else should die?
If not now, then when would be a better time?

My agitation lifted.
So did the fever.

Beneath every illness lies resistance.

Some say they need more time to practice,
thinking the Dhamma is akin to reading Proust.

The Dhamma does not need time.

If you can open your eyes you can practice the Dhamma.
Every waking moment is a gift for us
to practice awareness, equanimity and kindness.

Planning to take time for the Dhamma
is like waiting for the flood before you build a boat.

There is nowhere we need go.
There is nothing we need do.
The entire universe
dwells within us.
We hold all the mountains we need climb
and all the rivers we need traverse
in the palm of our hand.

Within my mind I find the cause of every war
and the source of every conflict.
And in my own heart lies
all the love needed to soothe these disagreements.

Going nowhere and doing nothing
I can accomplish everything because
when you do nothing, nothing is left undone.
Mountains are best climbed in full lotus.

The first thing you realize when you meditate
is just how crazy you are.
Your monkey mind runs the gamut from chaos to catastrophe.

Past injustices are re-visited and
future retributions plotted.
Love and kindness seem absent except
in their guises of guilt and remorse.

Do not fret. You are not going crazy…
you are already there.

You need only fret
when horrid thoughts arise
and you think you're fine.

Big men don't cry;
only the truly courageous do.
Big men hide behind the skirts of ego and bravado
but the courageous warriors of Dhamma
face the onslaught of outrageous fortune
with awareness and equanimity.
In doing so they are humbled to tears.

Only the strong and the brave can face enemies
with neither sword nor shield.
With truth in one hand and peace in the other
they fend off intimidation and pressure
by accepting their shrill cries
as simply the shock and awe of a desperate ego.

The timid retreat. The frightened attack,
but the brave do neither.
The brave don't need to do,
they are.

Problems abound.
Social, personal, political and financial conundrums beset the mind
fomenting a cauldron of agitation.
Trying to figure it out,
to work it out,
to get to the bottom of it
perpetuates the myth that the very thinking
that got us into the mess in the first place
will somehow free us.

And so we turn to meditation
to fuel the synapses of discernment,
to oil the rusty wheels of logic
and spark the light bulb
that will illuminate the way out of our labyrinth of options and
choices.

But meditation is not the way out either…
it is the way in.
Meditation solves nothing…
it dissolves.
It does not reveal answers…
it removes questions.

Opinions and judgments remain for sure
but we no longer side with ourselves.

Meditation is an opportunity to not work on our problems.
It allows us the time to not get anywhere
and the space to not do anything.

When nothing seems to be working
you are on the right track.

If it is with furrowed brow and clenched fist you sit,
pushing yourself, fervently hoping against hope
to end the suffering that is part and parcel of human life,
you will fail as miserably
as if you were pasting feathers together hoping for a duck.

You will point the finger of blame
at your teachers, at the technique,
at your fellow seekers, at your family,
at the environment, and your lack of time.

But you were bound to fail.
You were meant to fail.
You are hard wired to fall flat on your face until
you abandon all hope to succeed.

When you accept you cannot do it,
and only when you succumb to the impossibility
of conquering the Everest of the task before you,
are you really meditating.

Only then
with all your hopes for something better
dashed on the rocks of futility and despair,
does the brow unfurrow
and the fist unclench
and the pushing desists.

You simply sit.
You aren't conquering Everest.
Humbled before its majesty,

abiding in the futility of effort,
ask not for its blessing but for forgiveness
for your audacity to rise above base camp.
Egos conquer. Buddhas surrender.

There resides in all an inner voice.
A spirit guide, an angel or perhaps
a channeled ascended master
that speaks to your issues
and directs your quest.
This voice asks for your trust.

Don't listen to it.

It is wrong.
The beguiling voice
reflects only your desperate hope for easy solutions
and tempts you with your own polluted confusion.
It is the perfume of the painted harlot.

The voice you need heed
speaks the mist of the mountains.
It whispers the scent
of the dessert pines.
The silence of emptiness
echoes the teachings of the Tathagata
like a still forest pond
reflects the full moon.

Smaller Vehicle or Greater Vehicle?

The Way of the Elders roots out impurity
and replenishes the gaping hole with perfection.
Liberation is an achievement.

The Mahayana route cleans the dust
from our inherently enlightened mirror.
Liberation is a revelation.

Will it be excavation or decontamination?
Choose your metaphor but
be present and be at peace.

Choose a) or b)
but be,
eh?

Ultimately you are all alone.
All men are truly I-lands.

Still, you are not abandoned
nor without support.
All the powers and forces
for good and love and kindness
engulf and nurture you.

Though a shipwreck may best describe your life and
you may be hanging on to a life raft
with nothing in sight but a horizon of tomorrows,
the winds of Dhamma
and the tides of Metta
will eventually bring you to the far distant shore.

Your task is simply to stay on the raft
and trust the forces of nature.

The monks would meditate every afternoon
until the abbot released them for tea.
The highly sugared strong tea,
especially welcomed since no solid food was taken after twelve noon,
would sustain them during the long evenings.

One day the usual break time arrived
without the customary nod of emancipation from the abbot.
He remained deep in concentration.
The monks grew restless.
The abbot stayed steadfastly focused.
The monks' agitation grew though nary a one dared leave the hall.

Reconciled to their fate
the monks gradually settled into their own deep concentration
aware that more than an old abbot's forgetfulness was at play.
They felt a surge of adrenaline
as they were freed from their sugar and caffeine fixation.
They realized their tea break
was not a necessary component of the practice.
They smiled.
They opened their eyes to find the abbot smiling as well,
indicating his wordless discourse was complete.
He exited the hall.
The monks bowed and retired to their huts.

Years afterwards, when the monks were asked
about their master's greatest discourse,
they would remain silent.
After a prolonged pause they would reply,
"I guess you had to be there."

Sky is sky
whether clouds are gray or white.
Sky remains an empty, clear azure,
the clouds, floating far below the elegant expanse,
being more a by-product of the earth's dampness
than the sky's luminous grandeur.
The sky is not troubled by such fleeting, floating fluff.

Same with mind.
It is by nature crystal and clear.
Thoughts traverse the mind:
some gray, some white;
others dark and stormy.

Don't be afraid of thoughts.
Only take care lest your awareness of them be tardy.
After all these thoughts are not mind ...
nor mine.

Cling to nothing.
Why do you hold on to home,
to health, to family and friends,
to all that bring you hope?
This drive to control that which can't be controlled
unnerves and worries the mind
producing a state of perpetual ennui.

Cling to nothing by
letting go
not of health but fear of disease;
letting go
not of family but concerns for their future;
letting go
not of friends but of the worry of rejection;
letting go
not of enjoyment but the aversion to pain.

Your barn may have burned down,
but be happy,
now you can see the moon.

Is it the wind or the flag that blows?
The wind you say
for on a calm day
the flag lays limp.

True enough but it is also the flapping flag
that moves the wind.
Even the most passive of observers
alters that which he is observing.

Observer and observed dance,
entwined together,
each conveying the impression
that they alone are leading.

Pacifying our own mind
by altering our perception,
to see all things anew
changes the whole world
more than any army of the night.

Let the storms rage.
Let the winds roar
and the waves crash.

Still ponds fester and stagnate;
only raging waters can smooth a stone's rough edges.

I don't love anyone.
I don't love everyone.
I don't love you
and I don't love myself.
I don't love my family.
I don't love my friends.

I just love.

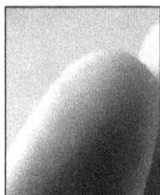

I cling; therefore I suffer.
The more I cling, the more I suffer.

Illness is less of a problem
than clinging to health.
Old age is less of a problem
than clinging to youth.
Poverty is less of a problem
than clinging to money.
Hunger is less of a problem
than clinging to food.
Unhappiness is less of a problem
than clinging to happiness.
Pain is less of a problem
than clinging to pleasure.

Life is less a problem
when you relinquish your hold.
You must learn to play the guitar
without strumming the strings.

In the name of the Dhamma you
arrange your life to maximize
the time and space you give to meditation.
You simplify. You modify. You delete.
Careers are terminated. Houses sold. Marriages cast aside.
You custom design your life like your morning latte.

But setting aside time and space just for Dhamma
is akin to scheduling blinking into your palm pilot.
The Dhamma requires not a change of clothes,
a change of jobs, a change of weather,
a change of address or a change of gears
but a change of mind.

The point of it all is to take down the prison walls,
not to make the cell more comfy.

You cannot crave what you already have;
you can only crave what you don't have.
Therein lays the misery.
Once you have what you didn't have
the craving, unquenchable and insatiable,
emerges again.

This person, this dream, this goal,
status, power, wealth
cannot assuage this gnawing hunger.
It doesn't work.
It has never worked.
It will never work.
It cannot work.

When craving is present...
and when is it not?...
it resembles the Trojan horse,
all haughty grandeur, inherently hollow,
but full of the force to overpower
your strongest resistance.

For the gypsy, it is a home;
for the householder, freedom.

When craving is simply noted
the gypsy finds he is already home
and the householder, forever free.

Learned scientists now tell us the Buddha was right.
Neurologists, physicists and psychiatrists
prod and poke and test,
electrify and verify and quantify,
and conclude that meditators are happier.

Don't believe them.
Don't believe the Buddha.
Don't believe this book.

Come and see for yourself.

The Buddha's message
is not found in his words,
nor in empirical research
and certainly not in this poet's mercurial meanders.

His message is in his smile;
its proof in yours.

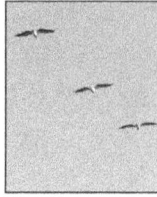

A man in far Mysore City garnered monies
by displaying his multi-hued parrots,
perched for petting and viewing
on a stick supported by two low trees.
The parrots, though untethered,
did not fly away.
He needed neither cage nor heavy hand
to extract their submission.

He had convinced the parrots
that their every need could only be met
if they remained quietly perched on the stick.

They didn't realize they could fly.
Their own fear held them firmly to that stick.

Freedom was theirs
if they just let go.

When left to its own devices
water naturally pools in the lowest gullies.
So it is with your mind.
Left on its own
thoughts meander hither and thither
eventually settling in the lower realms
wherein the darkest fears reside.

You immediately react when you uncover
this putrid cesspool of repressed fears,
your fear and ignorance darkening
your vision of the swamp even more.

Meditation allows you to calmly abide
in this quagmire of murky pestilence.
As you sit quietly
your eyes adjust to the light.
It is not so dark.
It is not so putrid.

There is no need to fear
what you don't want to know and
no need to flee from
what you don't want to face.

Shaking hands with the devil loosens his grip.

Trip the light fantastic
on feet of mirth and laughter.
Those guided by a child-like
sense of joy and wonder
have no need for the road map
of intellectual discernment.

An everlight heart smiles
at the curveball, low and away,
life throws our way.

We need not fear dropping the ball
if we never catch it in the first place.

Let it pass
as all things must.

Go against the mind.
If it says left, go right.
If it says eat, fast.
If it says sleep, work.
If it says, "I want", renounce
and when it says, "I hate", embrace.

The best time to sit
is when you are resisting the cushion's beckoning call.
Always listen to that little voice in your head...
and oppose it.

To meditate is more than noble:
it is imperative.
To desist from activity and just be
is profoundly energizing.
To refrain from engaging with any passing thought
is to immerse into everything.
To sit on your cushion,
to just sit,
is the embodiment of perfection.

To attend to this one breath,
just this one,
is to be, in this moment, a Buddha.

The challenge is to attend to the next breath as well.

Everyone seeks peace
imagining a freedom
from the mind-jostling volcanic eruptions
of greed and hatred.
Peace must be a zap-free zone,
devoid of nerve-grating negativities.

It is not so.
Peace is not so much a state
as a process.
Peace does not eliminate,
it accepts.
Peace does not obliterate
it welcomes.
Peace does not empty
it fills.

Peace opens your heart
to make room for all the mind states
we want so much to eradicate.
We calmly abide with
the disruptive forces allowing them to be as they are.
They need not be destroyed.

Though the impurities do not lose their identity
they do lose their density
and, like all scum,
they float to the surface
where they are evaporated
by the warm rays
of the Dhamma Dhatu.

Everything is changing.
Everything is always changing.
Everything is constantly always changing.
Everything is inherently constantly always changing.

This flux is more than the quintessence of the human condition;
it is the human condition.
You aren't a human being
as much as a human becoming.
To understand this at the visceral level,
in the heart, in the gut,
to fully grok it,
is to awaken to the ultimate truth.

You cannot step into the same river twice.
You cannot step into the river even once
for river is pure process,
an unfolding of riverness.

All one can be certain of is uncertainty.

My son likes the toy car at the mall.
He sits in the front seat and
places his hands on the steering wheel.
He works the pedals.
He can even honk the horn.
(And oh, how he loves to honk his horn!)
but he isn't in control.

He is just along for the ride
on the Kamma Express.

I am a torturer.
I am a rapist.
I am a jack-booted racist.

These beings live within me
and from time to time they raise their hands,
demanding recognition and asking to be heard.

When I fear these internal terrorists,
when I deny their existence,
when I repress their fury,
they win.
They get stronger.
They gather momentum.

Recognize them.
Call them by their name
and even befriend them.
But keep your eye on them.
Then they lose momentum.
They get weaker.
They implode.

The first step to being a better person
is to accept you are worse
than everyone else.

If you must wag your finger
do so at the image before you in the mirror.

The mind mirrors the body.
If the body moves, the mind moves.
If we still the body, we still the mind.
If we stop our breathing for even a moment,
the mind naturally calms.

Don't move.
Don't breathe.
Don't squirm, realign, fidget, slump, twist, turn, straighten, tilt, or
fall over.
Don't do.

Be.

Meditation is opening up to the obvious
and engaging the mundane.
We engross in the banal and the common.
It is earthworm knowledge.
We unload the silo
one grain at a time.

If you live the sacred and despise the ordinary,
you are still bobbing in the ocean of delusion.
If something magical is happening,
some miracle is unfolding
or some attainment has presented itself...
start again.

Expect nothing to happen
...and it eventually will.

Freedom may be the goal
but it is not the means.

Freedom as a means is
profligate indolence
hiding under the thin veneer of liberty.

The Path to freedom begins with effort and consistency,
undertaken with
discipline and determination
and augmented with renunciation and simplicity
before we reach liberation.

Nureyev soared on callused feet.

The Buddha exemplified balance.
He boldly set out for he knew not where
yet he was confident he would get there.
It appeared foolhardy to renounce his princely life
yet he was sure answers lay in the desert of renunciation.

You too need the courage to step into the void,
faithful that your foot will strike something solid.

Ready for anything;
expecting nothing.

Be aware.
Be awake.
If you think you are aware and awake
you are not.

If you think, you are
And you need to keep out of this.

No you turns in Dhamma.

The polluted mind reveals no wisdom.
It is all false leads circling back unto itself.
Smoke and mirrors. Shadows and fog.

We cannot think our way out of our quandary
much as we can't row a boat with a rotted hull
no matter how Olympic our stroke.
Thinking things through
gouges deep ruts into which we perpetually sink
leading us ever and anon over familiar turf.

Look to the mind beyond the quandary.
Look to the sky behind the clouds.
Look to the coral reef beneath the waves.

Don't let the quandary eat you up;
let it feed on itself.

Perplexity eats its progeny.

You dwell in a private garden of familiar discontent.
You wish for peace.
You wish for happiness.
You wish for joy eternal.
But these inhabit unfamiliar territory
beyond your garden's walls.
Best to stay within your incarcerating misery
and dream of better days
forever past or never to be.

You are addicted to your discontent.
It extends a kinship,
a familiarity,
a hazy, perplexing, consistent malaise
that you think is the real you.

You do not suffer.
Only the person you imagine yourself to be suffers.

Yours is a learned discontent
an engrained response,
deeply rutted in your unconscious.
You feel alive when this reactive pattern
surges through your veins
and you addict to the rush.

Your jaded myopia conceals
even the garden walls that confine you
let alone the door within that is always open
to the great clear beyond.

It's never too late to be what you might have been.

It is really so simple.
Watch and remain balanced.
Be present to all as it unfolds
neither wanting it to turn this way or that
nor angry should it not bend to your demands.
So simple.

It is really so hard.
Watch and remain balanced
to all and sundry, thoughts and events,
as they arise.
Seek neither lottery rewards nor fear crucifixion.
So hard.

The more we try
the harder it is.
The less we try
the simpler.

This thought that invades your consciousness,
this worry that swamps your being
or that desire that pinches you like a vice,
cries out for your total attention.
"Look at me" each spoiled brat screams,
"I need you here now!"

You have nurtured these errant thoughts and feelings
into petulant offspring by seating them front row, center stage.
You feed them, attend to them, stroke them, and empower them.
You are afraid to ignore them.
You need to deal with them.
Now.

You handed them the keys to the castle.
You made them the rulers.
You succumbed to their diatribes.
You prostrated yourself before the infantile wailing of envy and lust.

You need to regain control of your life.
You need to desist from rolling with each and every
bump and curve in the mindway.

You need to do nothing.

Like the flowers in a rainstorm
that bend and sway but remain firmly rooted
in clear awareness.

Hear their demands.
Hear their shrill screams
Listen to their supplications
but answer them not.

When these obsessive telemarketers call,
let the machine get it.

You who now are reading this
are a different person from the one who read the previous page.
You have changed.
Part of you has died
and part has been reborn.

You cannot relive the past;
you cannot revive your old self.
He who was, no longer is
and he who is, will not be he who will be.
You don't have to change;
you already have.

No need to turn over a new leaf,
to turn the corner
or turn your life around.
You have been turned…whether you like or not
and you were flipped sunny-side up.

Do not seek the truth.
Merely cease to cherish your own ideas and opinions.
Do not seek the truth
but continue truthfully searching.

You haven't lost anything,
nor is there anything you need find.
It is a goal-less goal.
The question is not "What are you looking for?"
but "Who is looking for what?"

You are looking for he who looks.
The truth is not so much found
as it is revealed.
And it is revealed by this very act of looking.
The act of looking is the truth.

When you look, you just simply see.
When you attend to the unfolding of reality,
as it is,
you have already found
what you thought
you were looking for.

It is all futile.
In the end, it is hopeless.
Even in the beginning, the struggle is a waste.
To realize this truth
without descending into despair
is Noble.

And Noble futility
will take you from befuddlement to
if not the cosmic,
at least the comic.

Never despair…
there is always hopelessness.

I struggled with a poem on compassion.
Words and images lay splattered on the page
like an ostrich egg under a fire truck.
Metaphors eluded my grasp.
Anecdotes migrated to far off isles.
Imagination lay stagnant
like so much still water on a moonless night.

My wife announced that she had invited friends for dinner.
"We could have discussed this first," I intoned,
my jab edged with patronizing sarcasm.
"I have some writing on compassion I must finish!"

It is futile to read these missives of Dhamma
without nurturing their inducements to a kinder life.
More futile yet is writing the missives in the first place
without heeding the teachings for
only he who acts wisely is so;
he who merely speaks wisely is just
another hawker in the spiritual supermarket.

The pen is mightier than the sword
but both pen and sword pale
in comparison with the gentle heart.

It is our attachments
that cause us pain.
Even our attachment to being unattached
is fraught with misery.
Better to be aware
when and if and how I am attached
than to be unaware
when and if and how I am not attached.

Let go of your misery for sure
but let go of your attainments even more.
Staring in amazement at how far you have come
is a sure sign you have much further to go.

Although gold dust is precious
when it gets in your eyes
it obstructs your vision.

Progress is not measured
by how far but by how still.

Over two millennia ago
the Buddha proposed the practice of dual tasking:
never awareness without equanimity
and never equanimity without awareness.

Equanimity and awareness
are the two wheels of a bicycle.
They are the two wings of the dove
forever linked in tandem like
rock and roll and
yin and yang.

Awareness is passing go;
equanimity is collecting $200.

Once you get past the fear,
the angst, the doubt
and the confusion,

watching

becomes a fascinating experience.

When there is no time line to which to adhere,
when there is no agenda,
when you want to neither eradicate nor induce

watching

thoughts, emotions, dreams and worries,
is like viewing a summer storm
from the cozy confines of a mountain cabin.

The Abbot came by the newly erected Dhamma hall
and inquired of his novice monks
how the project was progressing.

"It is all finished but the details,"
the youngest novice replied.

The aging Abbot shook his head.
"It is all only details," he murmured.

There is indeed no big picture,
no panorama of perfected harmony.
Looking to the heavens
lands us quickly in a quagmire.

It is a collage of minutiae,
of detailed filigree,
a panoply of pixels
to which you must pay attention.

It is not so much looking for the needle in the haystack
but looking at each piece of straw therein.

Sankhara.

These old familiar habit patterns,
born in the recesses of the antediluvian plain,
are destined to replay for eons upon eons,
ensnaring every thought, every emotion
in a miasma of interwoven cobwebs.

Your sankharas fit you
like a familiar baseball mitt.
Though you be buffeted and cajoled by them,
though you abhor their power
you are at the same time addicted
to responding in predetermined patterns.

They delude you
into thinking this is the way you are.
You may revel in knowing yourself
when it is only these habits you know
while your true nature lies obscured
beneath a blanket of blind bravado.
You are a perpetual mistaken identity.

These consistently reinforced reactive habits
have kidnapped your true nature
and demanded a ransom of lifelong obeisance.

You are the heir of your kamma.
This is your only inheritance.
You are as you did.
You will be as you are now doing.
What is past is indeed prologue.

The past isn't dead...
it isn't even past.

Renounce all that impedes your journey to the light
not out of stoicism, denial, hatred or superiority
but simply to separate needs from wants.

It is not "I will not,"
"I can not" or
"I must not"

but
"I need not."

"I need not at this moment indulge this whim"
releases you from the clutches of insatiable craving.
"Lagom" the Swedes say,
"just this is enough."

This is true freedom.
This is true liberation.

For he who desires nothing
everything seems a miracle.

The truth that sets you free
does not abide in the realm of pure reason.
It cannot be reached on flights of fanciful argument
nor through the thrust and parry of opinionated discussion.
The more we talk, the more we talk.

Truth is the way it is.
And the way it is
flashes before the mind's eye
in a kensho of clarity
after eons of effortless striving.

To see the truth is to understand the truth
and to understand the truth is liberation and so
our practice must lift
the veils of ignorance that obscure our vision.
Until we do so we remain engulfed in fog,
frantically rowing about,
in concentric circles of futility,
hopelessly lost, endlessly searching
unaware that this rowing about,
this fervent striving for escape,
leads only deeper into the morass.
The more we row, the denser the fog.

Truth that can be discussed is not the truth.

Meditation nurtures
how to know
when you know
there is no thing to know
except knowing this.

Meditation helps
you to find
what you never lost.

Just sitting
must be right sitting.
And right sitting
implies an investigative element
that propels meditation beyond the realm of relaxation
into the domain of insight.

Just sitting
must be true sitting.
And true sitting
implies a courageous honesty
to be fully present
to the arising and passing away
of mental conditionings.

Just sitting
must be simply sitting.
And simply sitting
implies a non-intellectual introspection
of the reality of here and now.

Just sit.
Right, true and simple…
so put the book down…
keep reading
but put the book down.

There must be more to life than speed.

When you live
a short distance from your body
in the state of constant modernity
involved with the to and fro,
perpetually preparing to really live,
you neglect the gifts of here and now.

When scintillating scenarios of anticipated hopes
act on the mind's stage or
when obsessions with past injustices and disappointments
demand retribution,
understanding cannot arise.

Open your heart
to the miracle of this simple moment.

Do not fret what was.
Do not plan what may be.

Do not expect even the next moment.

Sit as if you are viewing a play.

On stage sits anxiety.
What a good actor
able to stir up all matters mundane into tempests.
Doubt enters.
Like Shakespeare's Fool he comments on the very play itself
casting dispersion on the entire process.
As comic relief, here's joy
and what a relief she is. Pity she never stays long.
As usual, sadness follows her exit
bringing a pall over the entire play.

The usual actors come and go,
lurking sometimes in the background,
at other times charging to center stage.
When we identify so much with the actors,
relating to the conundrums and conflicts
into which they enter,
we surrender our ability to see the performances as just
so much smoke and fury,
ultimately signifying nothing.

We think the play's the thing
but it is mere illusion.

Only the viewers are real.

Lay it down.
Lay everything down,
persistently and consistently,
until laying down becomes
the new habit pattern of the mind.

It is not your burdens, however,
that you need lift off your shoulders;
nor is it your problems, woes or fears
that you need relinquish.

You need lay down your obsession,
your concern, your involvement with
your burden, your problems,
your woes, your fears.

Burdens are the stuff of life.
They are your inheritance
from your past actions.
They are real. They keep you human.
They are not heavy. They are your brothers.
They are also your teachers.

It is the desire to lay your burdens down
that adds the weight.

You must hold on while you let go.

Letting go occurs only when
you are holding tightly to here and now.
Sitting here, now,
trumps
standing there, then.

Letting go is not rethinking,
nor relieving, reviewing, rehearsing, replaying, reliving
but is real living
here, now,
with this breath.

Hold on tightly
but don't close your fist.

There is no greater teacher than
your worst nightmare.

Without your enemies,
and without fear of these same enemies,
where would you be?
Luxuriating in divine oblivion,
deluding yourself that you are
but one breath from liberation.

Your enemies make you uncomfortable.
They push your buttons.
They expose your prejudices and preconceptions
and uncover your most basic of tendencies.
Be thankful.

It is not what you know
but what you don't know about yourself
that deepens your practice
and this can best be revealed to you
by those you don't want to know.

Every moment you feel uneasy
a teacher is near and a lesson is unfolding.

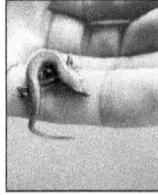

According to the traditions
of the forest monasteries of Issan
before a monk may leave the protective guidance of his preceptor
he must spend a night in the jungle,
alone and unsheltered.

Python, tiger and jungle cat abound here.
All are nocturnal hunters and all are hungry.
Monk sous l'arbre is a rare delicacy.

The monk takes a comfortable seated position under a tree,
vows not to move
and meditates through the night
emanating love and kindness
to protect himself from all manner of beast.

If and when he returns to the monastery,
with all extremities intact,
he will be freed from his vows of obeisance to his preceptor
having demonstrated that his love and kindness
is strong enough indeed
to fend off the destructive forces of Mara
and to warrant independence.

Monks have sat still, immersed in loving kindness,
as pythons slithered slowly over them.
A few in the morning have found
a jungle cat sleeping beside them.

Metta.
Don't leave home without it.

Cosmic consciousness having thus far eluded me,
I have settled for a state of comic consciousness
wherein irony reigns supreme and
hoisting myself on my own petard is the national sport.

I long for a cave in Issan
yet am happily ensconced in my suburban bungalow.
I love to hike the Himalaya
yet I drive my Volvo to the local market.
I write of the benefits of a strong spiritual practice
yet devour my weekly Sports Illustrated.
I march for peace
yet teach my son to box.
I live a life of quiet solemnity
yet prefer the Boss at full throttle.

I yam what I yam.
I do find my life quite funny.

Life occurs between a rock
and a hard place.
You are trapped between the rock
of being born
and the hard place of death.

You can choose to flee or to fight.
You can fly from reality
on drugged wings of sensual fancy
for momentary relief
or you can stand firm
on your religious convictions
that eternal deliverance is nigh.
Misery repressed with a scream of tortured excess
or with a howl of righteous indignation.

The Buddha suggested a middle way of
neither flight nor fight,
neither repression nor expression,
neither highway nor my way.

Simply sit between the rock and the hard place,
abide there calmly and just see what unfolds.
Expect nothing to happen…
and in time it will.

The Dhamma is not a spiritual practice.
It is not a feel-good,
ethereal, evanescent,
angels-dancing-on-a-pin,
pie-in-the-sky, warm and fuzzy
new age, psychotherapeutic,
Botox-for-the-mind.

It is a path for warriors.
Only the bravest of combatants
are willing to face the slings and arrows
of outrageous mental defilements
without retreating into morose anxiety
or suing for a complacent peace.

The path is laser straight.
It demands absolute 20/20 insight
of the reality of here and now.
You can't run and you can't hide.
The path offers neither escape nor exit.
The path is not a way out but a way in...
and ultimately through.

Before the dawn of liberation
you must face the dark night of your own entrapment.
And this you do alone,
with neither sword nor shield
but with the unshakeable knowledge
that it can be done,
it will be done
and it must be done.

The Dhamma is the ultimate reality show.
If you crave for the truth,
how is that different from pursuing
fame and riches?

If you don't seek the truth,
how different are you from
the fauna of the forests?

You must seek without seeking.
The truth can never be found by seeking,
yet only seekers find it.

Surrender to the hopelessness
of ever freeing yourself from the quicksand
of human frailty.

It is hopeless. You are helpless.
The direct help line to tech support
responds only after you hang up.

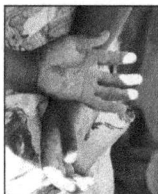

To err is human.
And to forgive may be divine
but true pardon falls short until you accept
that you also need forgiveness.
You too are preconditioned
to fall short of perfection.
You too are a victim of human frailty,
the universal human condition.

Only meditation can recondition
the precondition
of the human condition.

And it does so unconditionally.

By accepting the ubiquity of human frailty
you nurture empathy,
enabling you to recognize your own imperfection in others.
Seeing the universality of human frailty
transports us from the quagmire of self
to the heavens.
Sainthood is bestowed not on those whose heads are in the clouds
but on those whose feet slither in the mud.

If you weren't falling on your face
you could never see your fellow beings eye to eye.
Wisdom is oft times nearer when you stoop
than when you soar.

All alone,
all together.

I-lands unto ourselves,
unique constructs of preconditioning,
the beneficiaries of myriad past deeds,
and ultimately wholly responsible for our own unfolding,

we are yet all joined at the hip,
heart-linked together by human frailty
and the hope that spiritual salvation
awaits the good and the strong.

Paddling our own canoe
in others' choppy wakes.

The monk, Tenzin Gyatso by name,
walked with a stoop.
He had poor eyesight and constant pain
in his right leg.
His command of English left much to be desired.
He had no home.
And he had no country.

And yet he smiled.
His eyes danced with levity and mirth.
His happiness was infectious
and it underscored his message of peace.
He had only love for those who stole his homeland
and this love brought the largest nation in the world
to its knees.
He faced the largest army on earth
with naught else but a tender smile
and won the hearts and minds of the people of the world.

The soldiers may take his homeland.
They may destroy ancient monasteries.
They may imprison and torture countless countrymen
and they may even take his life.
But they cannot defeat him.
They cannot make him fight.
They cannot make him hate.

The strongest army is no match
for a smiling heart.

The entire universe is ruled
by cause and effect.
Every action
of every being
at every moment
results in a consequence.
And behind every action
of every being
at every moment
lies a thought.

As a man thinketh
so he is.
As a man thinketh
so is the entire universe.

Think about it ....

May I be well, happy and at peace.
May my wife be likewise well, happy and at peace.
May my sons grow up true and strong.
May my family be free from want.
May my friends be loving, kind and forthright.
May our leaders be honest, compassionate and wise.
May those who wish us harm be happy, calm and sympathetic.

May my door always be open to those in need of rest.
May my home always be open to those in need of sustenance.
May my heart always be open to those in need of love.

I forgive all those who may have hurt me
through their physical or mental deeds.
And I beg forgiveness from all those
whom I may have harmed
through my physical or mental deeds.

May all beings, male or female,
large or small,
two-legged or four-legged,
multi-legged or no-legged,
visible or invisible,
in this plane of existence
or another plane of existence,
be happy, be peaceful, be liberated.

When you meditate
you set aside time to distinguish
what is impermanent from what is not;
what is path from what is not;
and what nurtures happiness from what does not.

Like a good scientist you dissect and separate
the real from the apparent.
This is wisdom.
And like a good scientist you do so
with a serene detachment.
This is joy.

Meditation is not ascending above reality
but a burrowing into it.
We aren't eagles.
We are earthworms.

Meditation does not lead to truth.

Do not seek the truth.
Merely cease to cherish your own ideas and opinions.

Don't look for the truth,
because the looking is the truth.
No need to find what was never lost.

You aren't looking for the truth.
You are truthing.
All path. No destination.

There is no need to seek anything anywhere anyhow.
Enlightenment is not found by acquiring
but by letting go.

Walking on the beach
leaves no footprints.

What if you are realizing your dream?
What if you are exactly where you should be?
What if you are already the happiest person in the world?
What if you simply don't know that you know?
What if your dream of more is actually the nightmare from which
you are trying to wake?

More, not to mention most, is fraught with as much misery
as less, not to mention little.
There is no need to venture elsewhere.
Nothing you don't already have can make you any happier.
All you need to know is that a mountain is a mountain
and a river, a river.

A rich man is not one who has the most
but one who needs the least.

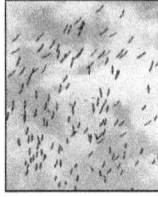

Thoughts are not the problem.
They are fleet-of-foot ephemera,
the wind in the willows of your mind.
Whenever you engage them
you anoint them with an oil of legitimacy
and bestow upon them a crown of permanency
they cannot wear.

Like painting the ebb and flow of the rolling seas,
you try to capture what has already passed on the mind's canvas.
You stare at your artistry
delighting in its grandeur,
reacting to blobs of blue paint while
the real waves have long passed on.

And you are left bobbing in their wake.

It is indeed difficult to find
your true self
since your true self is
neither true
nor your self.

Peeling away layer upon layer of the onion
leaves you empty-handed
and smelling badly to boot.
No inner onion exists.

Dismantling a watch
yields only wheels and gears and levers.
The watch cannot be found.

Truth and self
are the push-me pull-you
of your quest,
tugging you in opposite directions
for true self is the oxymoron of liberation.
What is true has no self
and what has self cannot be true.

What are you looking for?
Who is looking?
Why are you looking?

We look because that is what we do.
We are lookers.
We are seekers.
We are explorers.

What we are looking for
is who is doing the looking
and the who doing the looking
is just the looking itself.

No what. No who.
No why. No when.
No where. No how.
Know this.

The student gazed across the river
and saw his Master on the other side
seated under a cooling Banyan tree.

"Master," asked the student, "how do I get to the other side?"

"You are on the other side," replied the Master.

The Buddha became a Buddha when he realized
he was on the other side the whole time.

Whose side are you on?

Arguments abound
over the authenticity of texts.
Each school, each sect, each tradition
has very good reasons to believe
it represents the one and only path.

Their arguments are infallible,
their support irrefutable, and their conclusion solid
because logic and reason are on their side.
Each is right though
they are all wrong.

The one and only path
is simply the path that resonates with you.
Your own discoveries will support you
and your own insights will guide you.
Listen to everyone but heed no one's call.

The pundits and professors
reading, writing and arguing esoteric minutiae
yet who practice not
live in a virtual reality
generated by computer graphics
in a monastic Matrix.

I met a monk,
home to care for his ailing mother
after decades in the forest.
I too had surrendered solitary asceticism
for home and hearth
to marry and raise my sons.

"Big changes!" he said of my life.

"Big changes!" I replied about his.

Both of us had turned our lives 360 degrees around,
ironically finding ourselves flipped back onto the same path:
the path of love, equanimity, joy
and service.

Whether in the forest cave, at the hospital bed,
at the graveside or rocking the cradle
the practice of Dhamma remains the same.

Big change or little change or no change
we can all spare some change for those in need.

It was the last day of a meditation retreat.
During ten intensive days I guided the perplexed students
and answered their myriad questions.
I must say I did a most admirable job!

Assembled before me that last evening
were the servers and managers of the retreat.
I noticed the senior manager
tuck a Thank You card under her knee.

How unnecessary. How sweet.
Silently I reviewed my discourse on selfless service.
I would humbly mention that we received
no compensation, monetary or otherwise, for our work.
I was very proud of my lack of pride.
I would be well prepared to discourse on humility
when the Thank You card was presented to me.
If they loved me before the card …

We talked of preparations for the next morning
and we reviewed the week and what we had learned.
I said good night and waited, oh so humbly.
The senior manager stood, card in hand,
and left the hall with the other servers.

The card had not been for me.

I am not sure what message it contained
but it surely paled in comparison
to the one I received that evening.

What truth may be herein contained
lies not in the words
but in the spaces betwixt.
And it is to this emptiness,
to this silence,
to the quiet there
that we must turn to find the truth.

True, the pen is mightier than the sword
but stronger yet is the blank page,
open, simple and unadorned,
empty save for the focus of your attention upon its offering
of unbridled purity.

Silence is the perennial flow of language,
interrupted by words.
You need to be filled with this emptiness.

I no longer meditate in jungle caves
or sit for months in quiet solitude.
I have two sons now
and it is they who are my joyful focus.
I wear the vigilant visage of the harried parent
not the wane stare of the of the mountain hermit.
I measure my days in soiled nappies and teething rings.
Pali chanting no longer fills the air,
just the jingles of the Wiggles.
The Visuddhimagga has been shelved,
replaced by Goodnight Gorilla.
I seek not enlightenment but a quiet dinner.

All has changed and nothing has changed.
In leaving and returning
I remained at home.
This moment is still this moment.
This breath still goes in and then out.
I haul water. I hew wood. I change diapers.

I sit in quiet solitude
chasing my sons around the yard.

Don't meditate when you sit.

To meditate implies a technique, a method,
a particular skill of introspective intensity,
mastered by few,
taught by even fewer.

In truth it is nothing much.
It is just looking, within,
seeing what goes on behind your eyeballs.
It is paying attention to your inattentiveness.
Passive activity.
Engaged inertia.
Assertive atrophy.
Full throttle coasting.
Pedal to the metal parking.
Determined lethargy.

Learn to be silent.
Let your quiet mind
listen and absorb.

All man's miseries derive from not being able
to sit quietly in a room
alone.

You know before you know you know.
When you really pay attention
you become aware of subtle shifts of sensations
that arise before the rational mind engages.

You know when you feel the truth at a visceral level.
Intuition emerges, retrained and strengthened,
ready to guide and protect.

You already know the truth.
The Dhamma simply enables you to know you know.
Do you know that?

A father, hand-in-hand with his three year old son,
arrived one morning at our plastic sheeted, mud floored tea house
on Nhat Tha Gyi Pagoda Road.

They sat on low stools, drank their tea and ate their breakfast bread stick.
The father left on an errand
leaving his son alone at the table.
The boy drank his tea, ate his bread stick and watched the passing scene
of bare footed monks and school children,
rickshaw drivers and housewives.
Surrounded by friends and compatriots the young boy
appeared unperturbed by his father's absence.
Everything was aright in his universe;
he had tea, food and love.

But surely they need democracy.
They need the right to vote.
They need a free market economy.
They need Wal Mart.
They need to be more like us.

The father and son left the café after their breakfast.
They still were holding hands as I watched them turn the corner.
Poor wretched souls.

The double helix of DNA holds our genetic blueprint.
Blake held the entire universe in his hand.
And putting all his attention on one breath
the Buddha entered the deathless realm.

It seems that the smaller things get
the more truth they can hold.
Sometimes, we just need to be amazed by the small things.

A man came upon a poor frog stuck in the middle of the road.
The frog seemed immobilized by fear.
He gently scooped up the trembling frog
and carried him to the side of the road.
He stroked the frog and stepped back
to bask in the sunny glow of his charity and love
when the snake from whom the frog was escaping
emerged from the side brush and swallowed the frog whole.

Compassion must be married with wisdom;
otherwise its good intentions are devoured
by snakes in the grass.

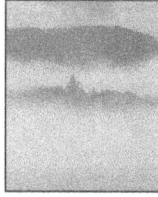

The miracle of meditation is not the answers we get
but the questions we relinquish.
Just as the nightingale's trill is muffled
under the tramping of our boots,
so too the sweet song of insight remains unheard
over the shrill call for answers.

You don't need to know any more;
you only need empty yourself of doubts and curiosity.

Stars come out to dance on the water
only after the fog dissipates.

Not everyone catches a wild turkey
but only a person who is actually running
can hope to do so.

Enlightenment comes only to he who
fervently pursues it
without expecting any success.

Strive earnestly and fervently,
prepared to lose every battle but the last one.
Like miners digging out a tunnel
one bucket of dirt at a time
sometimes we have no sense of progress.
Each bucket dug reveals another awaiting our attention.
Each bucket is given our undivided attention
without any hope or expectation
to break through to the other side.

Eventually
there is a breakthrough.
How did this final bucket
differ from the first?
Countless buckets to
reveal one thin sliver of light.

With awareness things are just as they are.
Without awareness things are just as they are.

Essence is immobile;
perception alone shifts hell
one-sixteenth of an inch
into heaven.

Equating the Dhamma with a technique of meditation
is akin to throwing away the apple
and eating the core.

If you can learn it,
if you can get good at it,
it isn't it.

Immortality is not living forever
but overcoming our fear of death.

Without fear
each day is an eternity;
and each night
a sleep fit for angels.

Today is not the first day of the rest of your life;
it is the only day of your life.
The secret is to live it to its fullest
as if it was any other day.
It comes but once in a lifetime.
Nothing special

This is what the Buddha knew.
When you know this
you too will be a Buddha.

Don't try to get somewhere
because then you would not be here.
Here is where you need stay
because there is but a projection
of your fear and hope.

Here is meditation…
elsewhere, trepidation.

Wishing things to be other than they are
is like pasting feathers together hoping for a duck.
No amount of hope, good will
or supplication to a higher source
is going to make it quack.

Knocking on heaven's door merely calcifies your knuckles.
All your prayers will be answered
when you get off your knees.

You can choose the path of the victim
or the path of the warrior.
The former begs for a life stolen from them;
the latter stands alone on the rocky cliff
and stares down the thieves of the night,
neither giving nor asking quarter,
until they reveal themselves
as only so much smoke and thunder
unable to steal what wasn't given to them in the first place.

The reclusive life in Himalayan caves
is exotic only to the accountant in Topeka.
Anyone who shuts their eyes
is a cave dweller.
And any mendicant who concerns
himself with the next moment
is a Kansas bookkeeper.

What is the use of reading all this poetry?
Your life, in all its dung-heaped majesty,
is poetry enough
for all the Buddhas.

Your free verse scans better
than another's iambic pentameter.

The Abbott was fond of encouraging his monks
with the Buddha's admonition,
"When eating, just eating.
When reading, just reading."

One day a novice found the Abbott reading a newspaper
while he ate his breakfast.
The quizzical look on the face of the novice
prompted the Abbott to reply,
"When eating and reading the newspaper,
just eating and reading the newspaper."

As I write these words
I pour a cup of tea and wonder,
"Who is this actor
who writes such drivel?"

Since the best you can have
is a mere image of yourself
how can you then decide
what you should or should not do?

This is like dining on sliced enigma dipped in fog
and wondering why you remain famished.

In Asia the practice of meditation
is stuck on form,
full of rites and rituals.

In America we have gone beyond form.
We have burned the Buddha images
and stripped ourselves of robes and chanting.
We are stuck in anti-form.

Form or no form
just sit straight.
Don't kill the Buddha
before you meet him.

Searching for happiness in riches and fame
is like digging in the ground
looking for blue sky.

Look upward,
above the clouds
for there the sky is eternally blue.

When I was young
we were so very poor.

We had sufficient food, of course,
a warm house
and good enough clothes
but other than that
we were so very poor.

Our entertainment was of the simple kind:
Saturday night hockey games,
Sundays and the Boy Scouts at Church
and long walks in the park.
We could afford naught else
for we were so very poor.

Perhaps our parents loved us,
coached our teams and
supported our dreams
all the more because
we were so very poor.

Not for us were trips to the Mall,
colored televisions or
dinners out
for these were beyond our kip.

When I was young
we were so very poor.
I am not so glad
my children can't say the same thing.

All religions are true
in the lies they tell.

This path or that,
it doesn't matter
for they all lead
to the same cul-de-sac.

Any truth that can be packaged
into a doctrine expounding
heavenly rewards and eternal damnation
overseen by the same God,
cannot be true.

If you can only believe it
and not experience it
you've missed it.

Do not mistake the finger
that points to the moon
for the moon itself.

Even a Buddha
can but show the direction;
he can't drop the destination
in your lap.

We tend to get caught up in the pointing ...
Whether it is a big or little finger,
a crooked digit or laser straight,
a prophetic or empirical gesture.

The path is clear
to those who can see.
Don't get waylaid
by the truckers' lights
at the side of the road.

You are all addicts.
You are all addicted to your drug of choice, be it
anger, lust, jealousy, pleasure, guilt, or worry.
Every interaction, every thought,
every sight, smell, touch, sound or taste
results in an all-so-familiar bio-chemical reaction,
an adrenaline-like secretion, which intoxicates you.
Unpleasant though it be, this surge of energy
is inevitably followed by momentary relief
when your anger is vented, your lust satisfied,
your jealousy requited, your pleasure realized,
your guilt assuaged, your worry abated.

You enjoy the anteceding unpleasant energy surge
because its ensuing release is so sweet.

You feel uneasy when you are at peace.
You fear tranquility.
Quietude is boring
because there can be no thrill of release from contentment.
You are so addicted to peaks and valleys
that you flee the plains below.

Live the Dhamma.
Proselytizers shout vacuities;
quiet minds model purity.

If this is the one and only path
there is no need to sell maps in the marketplace.
Walk the path and others will follow.

No need to let go.
Letting go is letting go
of the need to let go.

When the light is on,
there is no need to chase away the dark.

All things must pass.

All your thoughts, your judgments, your emotions
are passing fancies.
They are not you.
They are not even real
fabricated as they are by your own intrinsic
bias and trepidation.

What transforms this ethereal flux into mass,
what perpetuates that which is so fleeting,
what rejuvenates that which is on its way out
is your fear that this fleeting and exiting ephemera
may last forever.

Thoughts arise on the mind with a certain limited energy.
Left unattended they must eventually burn themselves out.
But you intervene, you intercourse and
interact with them
further fueling these unwanted states.
You empower what was
once a monologue creating a dialogue.
You are too polite to hang up.

There is no need to respond to unsolicited spam.

The first insight
arises when you uncover the horror hidden
in the deepest recesses of the mind.
Your delusions about your humanity,
your pretensions about your compassion and love
dissolve onto the mat beneath you.
These hellish visions
may overpower
revealing the real you to friends and family.

The second insight
arises when you discover that this horror show
is ephemeral.
It is not you.
It has no power.
It passes.

The trick is to persevere
between the two insights.
Keep on truckin'
though ever doubtful and anxiously concerned
you will never reach the second insight
before nightfall.

The highway between insights seems endless
but inevitably it passes
in a single breath.

Meditation is neither system,
nor technique nor way of thinking;
It does not reconfigure thoughts
into a sensible, discernable order.
You will not be smarter.
You will not be better organized.
You will not be thinner.
However, neither will you be the same.

Long breath, short breath;
deep breath, shallow breath.
Agitated mind, calm mind;
angry mind, peaceful mind.
The mind states are as they are.
Meditation does not orchestrate them
into a symphony of your choice,
but composes a simple wakeful presence
from the cacophony of dissonance.

Soup still stains your tie
but you recall only its bouquet.

When you first set aside
yesterday's regrets and tomorrow's dreams
to just abide in the now on your cushion,
the bliss you think you should be experiencing eludes you.
Your monkey mind jumps
from anger to hatred and lust to boredom
in the blink of an eye.

Congratulations!
You have burst the delusion
that you are pure and loving.
No longer can you hide this misconception
beneath the veneer of a smile and a glad hand.

You cannot heal what you flee.
Facing this truth must precede understanding the truth.
Most of the time what you face
is not pretty.
But better an enemy you know
than a friend you don't.

And the greatest enemy is the hidden one.

During long retreats I seemed to dance
with a different partner every day.
I have twisted with fear,
tangoed with anger
and jived with agitation.
Each new day brought a new dancing partner.

"Good morning Mara," I would say to myself upon arising,
"And with whom will I be dancing today?"
Soon my partner would introduce herself
and off we would go.

I insisted on leading.
My different partners would resist from time to time
wishing to set the tone and the tempo
but I remained steadfast and mostly enjoyed our spin on the floor.

Our practice must be a dance not a struggle.
And our training teaches us to lead.

Shall we dance?

You can't do it
because you and the it you think you want to do
are the same.
The looker and what is looked for
abide together in the act of looking.

No looker. No lookee.
Only looking.

Whither happiness?
Happiest is he who cares not a jot for the question,
knowing full well that attempting an answer
precipitates such agitation as to propel
him from heaven to hell in a single breath.

"Whither happiness?"
is a question
that sends you
looking in your jeans
for your La Traviata tickets.

Whither happiness?
I feel sorry for those who ask such a question;
even sorrier for those who have an answer.

When you bow raising calluses on your forehead,
light candles sufficient to land a 747,
or perform prostrations from Leh to Gaya
you are only paying respect
to the outward form of your practice.

Prostrate yourself, certainly,
but only if you aren't counting the number.
Light candles, of course,
but only if the electricity is out.
Bow, if you must,
but only until you're bowing,
even when you're not.

Index of First Lines

ABOUT PARIYATTI

Pariyatti is dedicated to providing affordable access to authentic teachings of the Buddha about the Dhamma theory (*pariyatti*) and practice (*paṭipatti*) of Vipassana meditation. A 501(c)(3) non-profit charitable organization since 2002, Pariyatti is sustained by contributions from individuals who appreciate and want to share the incalculable value of the Dhamma teachings. We invite you to visit www.pariyatti.org to learn about our programs, services, and ways to support publishing and other undertakings.

Pariyatti Publishing Imprints

Vipassana Research Publications (focus on Vipassana as taught by S.N. Goenka in the tradition of Sayagyi U Ba Khin)

BPS Pariyatti Editions (selected titles from the Buddhist Publication Society, co-published by Pariyatti in the Americas)

Pariyatti Digital Editions (audio and video titles, including discourses)

Pariyatti Press (classic titles returned to print and inspirational writing by contemporary authors)

Pariyatti enriches the world by

- disseminating the words of the Buddha,
- providing sustenance for the seeker's journey,
- illuminating the meditator's path.

www.ingramcontent.com/pod-product-compliance
Lightning Source LLC
LaVergne TN
LVHW011236080426
835509LV00005B/525